THE COMPLETE BAR/BAT MITZVAH PLANNER

Linda Seifer Sage

St. Martin's Press
New York

Originally published by Danscott Publishing under the title *The Bar Mitzvah and Bat Mitzvah Easy Planner,* 1991.

Although the author has researched numerous sources to ensure the accuracy and completeness of the information contained in this book, she assumes no responsibility for errors or omissions. Any slights against people or organizations are totally unintentional.

Please address all correspondence to:
Linda Sage
14 Evergreen Row
Armonk, New York 10504

Book Design and Typesetting by Ken Hamilton

Library of Congress Cataloging-in-Publication Data

Sage, Linda Seifer.
   The complete bar/bat mitzvah planner / Linda Seifer Sage.
    p.   cm.
   ISBN 0-312-09260-1
   1. Bar mitzvah etiquette—Handbooks, manuals, etc. 2. Bat mitzvah
   etiquette—Handbooks, manuals, etc. I. Title.
   BJ2078.B3S24   1993   93-14857 ✓
   395'.24—dc20   CIP

June 1993

10 9 8 7 6 5 4 3 2 1

Printed in United States of America

Contents

Countdown

Reception

Entertainment

Photography/Videography

Dedication

My son, Daniel, told me that the day of his Bar Mitzvah was the best day of his life. I would like to dedicate this book to him and also to my younger son, Scott. Dan made me such a proud parent on that day, and I know Scott will make me just as proud on his Bar Mitzvah day. Of course, I also must thank my husband, Don, for without him I could not have these wonderful moments in life to remember and cherish forever.

Acknowledgments

I'd like to thank everyone who helped make this book possible. For moral support, I'd like to thank my biggest fans: my mom; my sons, Dan and Scott; and my friends Donna Spiegel, Joan Addessi, Carol Santora, Alice and Joe Perdue, Janice Price, Dukie Baxter, Judy Novenstein, Rowena and Don Dery, and Sue Madris, whose proofreading skills proved to be invaluable. These are the people who are always in my corner, encouraging and cheering me on to succeed, whatever my latest venture. Thank you also to my cousins, Joanne and Mike Grabow, who first showed me that planning a Bar Mitzvah celebration can be one of the happiest times in my life.

For his expertise, I'd like to thank George Cochran, a shining star of enthusiasm; Bill Golub for his professionalism; Barbara Bergeron, my very capable copy editor; and Matt Forner of BookCrafters.

Certainly I can not overlook thanking my Rabbi, David Greenberg, for without him the day of my son's Bar Mitzvah could not have been such a joyous, special and momentous occasion.

Most of all, this book surely would not have been possible without my guardian angels, Marian and Ken Hamilton. Marian capably guided me through the production stage, having just completed her comprehensive guidebook *"The Best of Westchester"*, and Ken offered his own expertise in design and typesetting. The time he put into this was well beyond the call of duty.

Last, but not least, I want to thank my husband, Don, for his encouragement and patience and because he is my most ardent supporter, best critic, confidant, and always my very first editor.

Thank you all once again.

Introduction

The Bar or Bat Mitzvah day of your son or daughter should be a very special day for your entire family. It's a day you'll all want to enjoy fully—not a day when you are so overwhelmed by plans for the service and party that you are more exhausted than excited. This workbook was designed to help. It was developed from my own trial-and-error experience planning my son's Bar Mitzvah. Numerous people have since used it and were kind enough to contribute suggestions and advice based on their own experiences. Each one of us remembers things we forgot to do or wished we hadn't done. With the help of this workbook, you'll be able to learn from all of our mistakes. Why should you forget to have that special picture of Nana Muriel dancing with her grandson on his special day?

I started by keeping lists of all the things that I needed to do. The more checklists I made, the easier it was to be organized. This planning workbook will help you to keep track of addresses, telephone numbers, appointments, costs, and decisions that need to be made. You will also see, as you fill it in, how much easier it is when everything you need is in one place. Take the workbook with you as you visit caterers, photographers, florists, etc. Write everything down so that you won't have to rely on your memory. It'll be much easier to compare prices and review what's included or not included later on when you return home. Write in pencil so that you can erase. Check items off as they are completed. This will give you a feeling of accomplishment as less and less remains to be done. Best of all, it will free you from all worrisome details so that you and your family can have a relaxing and wonderful day with everything going exactly the way you planned.

If you have any comments, questions or suggestions, I'd love to hear from you. You can write to me at 14 Evergreen Row, Armonk, N.Y. 10504. Until then, happy planning!

Countdown

Countdown to the Big Day

One- to Two-Year Countdown   **Done?**

Decide on Date and Time _____

Plan Budget _____

Choose Reception Location _____

Choose Caterer _____

Select Band/Disc Jockey _____

Decide on Other Entertainment _____

Six-Month to One-Year Countdown

Choose Mother's Attire (need time for alterations) _____

Select Florist _____

Select Photographer _____

Select Videographer _____

Select Decorator or Party Planner _____

Order Sign-In Board (if ordering from artist) _____

Four-Month Countdown

Prepare Guest List _____

Select Printer _____

Select/Order Invitations, etc. _____

Design Maps/Write Directions/Order _____

Select Favors _____

Arrange for Rentals _____

Three-Month Countdown

Choose Father's Attire _____

Choose Bar/Bat Mitzvah Attire (not too early — growing) _____

Choose Siblings' Attire _____

Address Invitations _____

Order Favors _____

Order Cocktail Napkins, Guest Towels, Yarmulkes _____

Two-Month Countdown   Done?

Set Date to Meet with Rabbi _____

Order Cake (make delivery arrangements) _____

Mail Invitations _____

Buy Gifts for Rabbi, Cantor/Choir _____

Make Hairdresser/Nail Appointments_____

Give Temple Information for Personalized Booklet _____

Make Hotel Arrangements for Out-of-Town Guests _____

One-Month Countdown

Plan Exact Menu with Caterer (including cake) _____

Meet with Rabbi_____

Arrange Transportation for Children/Out-of-Town Guests_____

Order Challah (if caterer not doing it) _____

Make Final Arrangements with Florist/Give Directions _____

Make Final Arrangements with Band/DJ and Give Directions _____

Meet with Photographer/Give Instructions and Directions _____

Meet with Videographer/Give Instructions and Directions_____

Speak with Decorator to Reconfirm Plans/Give Directions_____

Have Child Write Speech and Practice in Front of You_____

Decide on Table Assignments/Number of Centerpieces _____

Write Place Cards/Alphabetize _____

Wrap Favors for Children _____

Have Men Get Haircuts (sometime during month)_____

Prepare Checklist of Last-Minute Reminders_____

Some of these items may be completed at the last moment but the more you can do in advance, the more relaxed you'll be as this special day approaches. Check each item off as you complete it.

Checklist of Last-Minute Reminders

Remember to Bring to Temple   Done?

    Yarmulkes, Tallis _____

    Challah, Cakes, Wine (if caterer not providing) _____

    Small Cups for Wine, Napkins_____

    Platter, Bread Knife _____

    Copies of Aliyah _____

    Extra Direction Cards to Reception Location _____

    Child's Speech/Hebrew and English Portions _____

    Parents' Prayer _____

    Rabbi/Cantor/Choir Gifts _____

Remember to Bring to Reception   Done?

    Sign-In Board, Easel, Several Pens or Markers _____

    Favors_____

    Place Cards _____

    Seating Arrangement _____

    Prizes for Games _____

    Extra Challah (if caterer isn't bringing) _____

    Cash for Tips (e.g., bartender) _____

    Checkbook/Checks Made Out_____

Time Schedule

Event   **Approximate Time**

Family Arrives at Temple _____

Guests Arrive at Temple _____

Service Begins_____

Kiddush Begins for All Attending Service _____

Guests and Family Leave for Reception Location _____

Guests and Family Arrive at Reception Location _____

Cocktails and Hors d'Oeuvres Are Served _____

Luncheon/Dinner Begins_____

Reception Concludes _____

Reception

Selecting Your Date

You will be receiving the date for your child's Bar or Bat Mitzvah as much as two years in advance. How much in advance will depend on your specific temple. The date you are given can be changed if necessary.

You should definitely consider changing the date if it conflicts with another Bar/Bat Mitzvah. For example, suppose another child in your son's school, who belongs to a different temple, is given the same date. You might think it doesn't matter. My son, you think, isn't really friendly with him. Later you discover that this other child's invitations were sent out several weeks before yours. Many children on the guest lists for both will accept the first invitation immediately, unaware that yours is coming. This may not bother you, but it may disturb your child. Friends will have to choose which party to attend, making it into a popularity contest. You and your child do not need this additional anxiety.

If the other child's invitation is for a Bat Mitzvah and yours is for a Bar Mitzvah, there will still be problems. Usually, most of the girls will go to the Bat Mitzvah and most of the boys will go to the Bar Mitzvah. This eliminates the children's dancing at both parties!

To avoid this conflict, consult other temples in your area to find out what Bar and Bat Mitzvah services are scheduled on your date. Most are very happy to help. In addition, your own temple will usually do everything possible to find a date that you are happy with for this special occasion.

Selecting Your Time

At most temples, your choice for the service is either Saturday morning or late Saturday afternoon. The late Saturday afternoon service, a Havdalah service, is only permitted at some temples. Since the exact time and length of the service vary from temple to temple, it is wise to attend a Bar or Bat Mitzvah service at your own temple so that you will know precisely when it begins and ends.

When informing the caterer of the time you expect your guests will begin arriving at the reception, don't forget that it is customary to have a kiddush at the temple for your guests and members of the congregation after the service. Also, consider travel time from the temple, if the reception is being held somewhere else. Most restaurants, clubs and caterers will assume you will want one hour for cocktails and hors d'oeuvres and four hours for the meal. Knowing the exact times will help you to properly plan your day.

There are numerous times you can have your reception. Most often it is immediately following the service in the afternoon or Saturday evening. Many people choose to have it in the afternoon because they feel it is probably more convenient for their guests, especially when small children are invited. Others decide that this time span between the ceremony and the reception is unimportant. They feel that Saturday evening is more festive and music is permitted. (Some temples do not permit music in the synagogue on the Sabbath.)

On occasion, various other times are chosen for the Bar/Bat Mitzvah. Sunday is sometimes selected because it enables Orthodox guests, who will not travel on Saturday, to attend.

Selecting the Place for Reception

The place you select for your reception has to be booked one to two years in advance. I know it seems ridiculous to plan so far ahead, but you do have a lot of competition. There are many people out there, just like you, looking for that perfect place, and there are a limited number of possibilities in your area. These people are not only planning Bar and Bat Mitzvah celebrations, they are also planning weddings and various corporate and charitable affairs.

If you already know exactly where you want to have your reception, reserve the place with a deposit as soon as you get a date from your temple. This is one way to save yourself a lot of aggravation. Of course, you can usually reserve your temple reception area with less notice. More and more temples, however, are permitting non-members to rent their facilities, so you'll still have to make your decision quite some time before the Bar/Bat Mitzvah date.

A Restaurant

If you have a favorite restaurant that is large enough, and has great food, it may be perfect. In addition, you are probably already aware whether or not they have good, efficient service. Also, many restaurants provide their own flowers in the foyer and on the tables, certainly a good way to save on decorator costs if you intend to keep it simple. Don't forget about restaurants in hotels, especially if there is a good one in the hotel where your out-of-town guests will be staying.

The one big drawback with restaurants is that many will not allow you to have your party on a Saturday evening because this is when they do their best business. Some, however, do have private rooms. Having an afternoon affair can also be a bit tricky because you may be asked to vacate the restaurant by 4:30 p.m. so that the staff can prepare for their own clientele. This can become awkward if your guests are still dancing and having a great time.

The Club

This can be ideal. If you don't belong to one, consider asking a friend to sponsor you. Clubs usually will book only one affair per day so you won't be pushed out at a specific time; you and your guests will have the entire place to yourselves. In addition, you or your friend will be familiar with the food and service. You can also take comfort in knowing that the staff will want to please you and your guests since they know they will have to face you again and again in the future.

The Temple

This is probably the easiest and most convenient reception location for your guests since no one will have the hassle of traveling after the service. Also, you don't have to worry about providing transportation for out-of-town guests and children unaccompanied by parents. However, you will have to consider when music is permitted to be played, the acoustics of the social hall, non-kosher food restrictions, the size of the temple social hall, and the adequacy of kitchen facilities.

The Catering Hall

The biggest drawback with catering halls is that most have several affairs going on simultaneously. This may or may not bother you; it really depends on your feelings about having a private party. Another possible shortcoming with large catering halls is that they may have several staffs, providing inconsistent food quality and service. References about the food or service could then mean nothing! Don't assume that they have a permanent staff—ask! Check to see exactly who you are getting.

Home Sweet Home

If your house has sufficient room, or there is enough space outside to erect a large tent and your date is during the spring or early fall, this may be a choice you will want to consider. Having the reception in your home is especially appealing if you know a caterer who will serve great food. When hiring a caterer, though, find out exactly what you and the caterer are responsible for doing. Some will provide only the food, while others will include service, linens, tables, china, silverware, and clean up. Don't forget about clean up! If you decide to use a tent, you may also have to rent a dance floor, lights if it's at night, and heaters if chilly weather is possible. Keep in mind here that although the food may be great, the service may not be. Make sure you get several references and ask questions about the staff. How experienced are they? Is it their permanent staff? An alternative to having a caterer is for you to do the cooking, but I recommend this only if you have a very small guest list, can prepare all the food in advance, have a huge freezer, and plan to hire a service crew that you know is reliable.

Finally, if you decide to have your affair at home, keep in mind that this decision may involve your spending time fixing up your house. Then again, this party could give you the inspiration and incentive to finish all those projects you always wanted done around the house anyway.

Instructions to Caterer

Cocktail Hour

Give the caterer an approximate arrival time. Tell him how long you would like the cocktails and hors d'oeuvres served (usually one hour). Be very specific as to which hors d'oeuvres you would like passed by waiters to your guests and which you want on the hors d'oeuvres table (e.g., cheese, crackers, stuffed cabbage). If you expect everything to be plentiful, you'd better say so. Otherwise, you may find yourself very disappointed when the hors d'oeuvres are rather scanty.

Lunch/Dinner

Select your appetizer, salad, dressing, rolls, main course, sauces, and vegetables. Most caterers will give you only one main entree selection. If Uncle Rick is a vegetarian or there are other guests who need special meals, determine in advance what you will be charged. Most caterers will have some sort of choice for your guests who can't eat the entree you've selected. However, caterers won't allow more than a dozen or so of these meals because it is just too costly to them to permit each guest to make a selection—unless, of course, you are willing to pay for this option. Don't forget that for some of your guests, you may also have to order kosher meals from a kosher restaurant or caterer. Sometimes the children are served an entirely different meal than the adults (e.g., hamburgers or fried chicken). If this is the case, there should be a totally different price for their meals. Finding a caterer who will give you a fair price on the children's menu can really save you a lot of money since one-third of your guests may be children.

If you really want to have an affair that doesn't cost a fortune, consider a buffet. You will have to find a caterer who has great food, is willing to offer your guests a selection of several dishes, and doesn't charge you the normal extraordinary per person price because much less service is needed.

The Open Bar

What this usually means is that all of your guests can have as much to drink as they want, normally for four hours, for a fixed price. You may like this arrangement if you believe your guests will consume a lot of alcohol or you don't want to be surprised by a large bar bill at the end of the affair. However, if you feel that the bartender can keep an accurate count, you'd probably save a lot if you didn't have an open bar. People are drinking a lot less these days because they are concerned about drinking and driving and about the calories in drinks. Remember, with an open bar, it doesn't matter that Aunt Betty doesn't drink at all or that half your guests are on diets and have diet sodas. You will be charged as if each of your adult guests has four or five drinks each! So, if the place you are having your affair permits it (some don't), you may want to consider paying by the drink. There are also places that will permit you to purchase the liquor yourself and then pay them only for set-ups and service.

Make sure you decide with the caterer exactly how the children will be served during the cocktail hour. You shouldn't be charged for an open bar for them too, but many caterers do this. You may want a separate bartender to serve the children soda or juice concoctions or a separate children's table set up with drinks.

Challah

Make sure you know who is going to bring the challah, you or the caterer. An assumption is made that the caterer will take care of this for you, which he often does, but you had better check. What you normally see in most bakeries is the single challah. If you want the double one, for the traditional slicing of the challah at the temple and at the reception, you'll have to order them yourself. It requires an advance order of only a couple of days at most, but it's an item that's often overlooked. You may also want to purchase a couple of extra challahs so that everyone can have a slice at temple and some at the reception. The challahs can be cut up and placed on tables in baskets so everyone can have a taste.

Dessert

Some caterers include a cake and/or a dessert, some do not. You may prefer to purchase your own cake, if you know a bakery that will do a special job for you. Also, decide if you will be serving only the cake for dessert or serving everyone a token piece of cake in addition to a dessert served by the caterer. Sometimes the children are served one dessert and the adults are served another. Perhaps the children will have a make-your-own-sundae table while the adults choose from various other dessert selections (Viennese table). Each of these alternatives makes a difference as to what your final price per person will be.

Candles

Another item sometimes overlooked, would you believe, is the candles. Again, speak to your caterer about this. If you are having the traditional candle-lighting ceremony, you won't need that many, but if you are going to have the "big blowout," you'll need one for each of your guests, in addition to those on the cake. The "big blowout" occurs when the immediate family stands together in front of the cake as each of their guests is given a candle. A waiter walks around and lights one candle at each table, and the guests then use this candle to light the rest of the candles at the table. Finally, the thirteen candles on the cake are lit (the last one by the

Bar/Bat Mitzvah), "Happy Birthday" is sung, and all the candles are blown out.

Other Arrangements

If you are providing the cake yourself, also arrange for the delivery. Make sure the bakery notifies the club or restaurant so that someone will be there to receive it and room is provided in their refrigerator or freezer (if the cake is quite large). If you want anything moved in the reception area (e.g., piano for cocktail hour), make sure you mention it beforehand. Or, if there is any furniture or paintings you dislike and want removed for your affair, mention that too. Assume nothing.

Give the caterer the color you want for the linens and napkins (most have a selection of colors) and find out if floor-length linens can be provided, if that is what you prefer. Caterers can really get carried away here, so be careful. They may charge you for different colors and different lengths, unless you select what they already have. Usually, then, there is no charge. You can also ask them to fold the napkins in a special way (there is usually no charge for this service).

Decide if you want the adults or children served first. It's not a bad idea to serve the children first since they eat so quickly. Then you can have the band or DJ play games with them while the adults dine. This way you can avoid having loud music playing while people are eating and wish to converse.

Payment

Normally, you will have to give the caterer a deposit to hold your date. Be sure to find out under what conditions it is refundable. The rest will be billed to you afterwards. The caterer will want to know sometime during the week before your affair the exact number of guests. You may want to give as a "final count" a few people less than your total number of accepted invitations. You can always add on, but you will definitely pay for whatever number of guests you give them, even if someone cancels at the last minute. Also, once again, don't forget to get a separate price for the children's meals. It should be a lot less if you are having a totally different menu for them and, of course, no open bar. Unfortunately, all-too-many caterers won't give you this benefit.

Reception Location/Caterer Possibilities*

Name:_____   Deposit:_____

Address: _____   Balance Due: _____

Telephone: _____   Gratuities:_____

Min./Max. Guests: _____   Service/Guest Ratio:_____

Manager: _____   Time Available: _____

Details:

Menu Selection/Price Range _____

_____

_____

_____

Children's Menu/Price/Age Cutoff_____

_____

Substitute Menu_____

Linens/Length/Colors/Included _____

Dessert/Cake/Challah/Candles Included _____

Open Bar/Per Drink _____

Tables for Place Cards and Gifts _____

Easel for Sign-In Board _____

Attendants/Check Room/Parking _____

Restrooms/Location/Condition _____

Accessible to Handicapped Guests_____

Deposit/Refundable _____

Other (e.g., easy to work with, knowledgeable) _____

References_____

_____

_____

*Call first to see if available on your date; this saves a lot of
legwork. For your convenience, duplicate forms are included for each of your interviews with caterers.

Reception Location/Caterer Possibilities

Name:_____   Deposit:_____

Address: _____   Balance Due: _____

Telephone: _____   Gratuities:_____

Min./Max. Guests: _____   Service/Guest Ratio: _____

Manager: _____   Time Available: _____

Details:

Menu Selection/Price Range _____

_____

_____

_____

Children's Menu/Price/Age Cutoff_____

_____

Substitute Menu_____

Linens/Length/Colors/Included _____

Dessert/Cake/Challah/Candles Included _____

Open Bar/Per Drink _____

Tables for Place Cards and Gifts _____

Easel for Sign-In Board _____

Attendants/Check Room/Parking _____

Restrooms/Location/Condition _____

Accessible to Handicapped Guests_____

Deposit/Refundable _____

Other (e.g., easy to work with, knowledgeable) _____

References_____

_____

_____

_____

Reception Location/Caterer Possibilities

Name:_____   Deposit:_____

Address: _____   Balance Due: _____

Telephone: _____   Gratuities:_____

Min./Max. Guests: _____   Service/Guest Ratio:_____

Manager: _____   Time Available: _____

Details:

Menu Selection/Price Range _____

_____

_____

_____

Children's Menu/Price/Age Cutoff_____

_____

Substitute Menu_____

Linens/Length/Colors/Included _____

Dessert/Cake/Challah/Candles Included _____

Open Bar/Per Drink _____

Tables for Place Cards and Gifts _____

Easel for Sign-In Board _____

Attendants/Check Room/Parking _____

Restrooms/Location/Condition _____

Accessible to Handicapped Guests_____

Deposit/Refundable _____

Other (e.g., easy to work with, knowledgeable) _____

References_____

_____

_____

_____

Reception Location/Caterer Possibilities

Name:_____   Deposit:_____

Address:_____   Balance Due:_____

Telephone:_____   Gratuities:_____

Min./Max. Guests:_____   Service/Guest Ratio:_____

Manager:_____   Time Available:_____

Details:

Menu Selection/Price Range _____

_____

_____

_____

Children's Menu/Price/Age Cutoff_____

_____

Substitute Menu_____

Linens/Length/Colors/Included _____

Dessert/Cake/Challah/Candles Included _____

Open Bar/Per Drink _____

Tables for Place Cards and Gifts _____

Easel for Sign-In Board _____

Attendants/Check Room/Parking _____

Restrooms/Location/Condition _____

Accessible to Handicapped Guests_____

Deposit/Refundable _____

Other (e.g., easy to work with, knowledgeable) _____

References_____

_____

_____

_____

Reception Location/Caterer Possibilities

Name:_____ Deposit:_____

Address: _____ Balance Due: _____

Telephone: _____ Gratuities:_____

Min./Max. Guests: _____ Service/Guest Ratio:_____

Manager: _____ Time Available: _____

Details:

Menu Selection/Price Range _____

_____

_____

_____

Children's Menu/Price/Age Cutoff_____

_____

Substitute Menu_____

Linens/Length/Colors/Included _____

Dessert/Cake/Challah/Candles Included _____

Open Bar/Per Drink _____

Tables for Place Cards and Gifts _____

Easel for Sign-In Board _____

Attendants/Check Room/Parking _____

Restrooms/Location/Condition _____

Accessible to Handicapped Guests_____

Deposit/Refundable _____

Other (e.g., easy to work with, knowledgeable) _____

References_____

_____

_____

_____

Reception Location/Caterer Possibilities

Name:_____   Deposit:_____

Address: _____   Balance Due: _____

Telephone: _____   Gratuities:_____

Min./Max. Guests: _____   Service/Guest Ratio:_____

Manager: _____   Time Available: _____

Details:

Menu Selection/Price Range _____

_____

_____

_____

Children's Menu/Price/Age Cutoff_____

_____

Substitute Menu_____

Linens/Length/Colors/Included _____

Dessert/Cake/Challah/Candles Included _____

Open Bar/Per Drink _____

Tables for Place Cards and Gifts _____

Easel for Sign-In Board _____

Attendants/Check Room/Parking _____

Restrooms/Location/Condition _____

Accessible to Handicapped Guests_____

Deposit/Refundable _____

Other (e.g., easy to work with, knowledgeable) _____

References_____

_____

_____

_____

Menu

Cocktail Hour

Hot Hors d'Oeuvres	Cold Hors d'Oeuvres

Luncheon/Dinner

	Adult	Children	Substitute (kosher, vegetarian)
Appetizer			
Salad/Dressing			
Rolls/Bread			
Main Course			
Vegetables			
Dessert			
Beverage			

Bar

(Open or Per Drink)

	Variety	Amount
Champagne		
Wine		
Beer		
Liquor		
Set-ups		
Soda		
Diet Soda		
After-Dinner Drinks		

Food/Bar Costs

	Number	x Cost/Person	= Total
Adults			
Children			
Substitute			
Bar			
		Final Total	

Equipment Rental*

Item		Number	Description	Cost
Tent				
Dance Floor				
Tables	60"			
	72"			
Chairs				
Heaters				
Lights				
Silverware				
China				
Glasses				
Linens	60"			
	72"			
Trays				
Other				

*For any equipment rental, see what you are getting. You don't want stained linens or uncomfortable chairs.

Additional Purchases

Item	Number	Description	Cost
Cocktail Napkins			
Place Cards			
Guest Towels			
Matches			
Candles			
Yarmulkes			
Other			

Staff to Hire

Description	Number	Uniform	Cost
Bartenders			
Waiters/Waitresses			
Busboys			
Other			

Reception Schedule of Events*

First Hour

(e.g., guests arrive, cocktails, hors d'oeuvres, music begins, entertainment):

_____

_____

_____

_____

_____

_____

After First Hour

(e.g.,family announced, guests seated, challah blessing, traditional hora, candle lighting with music accompaniment, children served, adults served, children's games, other entertainment, toasts made, other):

_____

_____

_____

_____

_____

_____

_____

_____

_____

_____

_____

_____

_____

_____

*Schedule events in order of preference and give a copy of
the schedule to band/DJ and caterer. Copies are included
here for your convenience.

Reception Schedule of Events

First Hour

(e.g., guests arrive, cocktails, hors d'oeuvres, music begins, entertainment):

_____

_____

_____

_____

_____

_____

After First Hour

(e.g., family announced, guests seated, challah blessing, traditional hora, candle lighting with music accompaniment, children served, adults served, children's games, other entertainment, toasts made, other):

_____

_____

_____

_____

_____

_____

_____

_____

_____

_____

_____

_____

_____

_____

Notes

Reception Schedule of Events

First Hour

(e.g., guests arrive, cocktails, hors d'oeuvres, music begins, entertainment):

_____

_____

_____

_____

_____

_____

After First Hour

(e.g.,family announced, guests seated, challah blessing, traditional hora, candle lighting with music accompaniment, children served, adults served, children's games, other entertainment, toasts made, other):

_____

_____

_____

_____

_____

_____

_____

_____

_____

_____

_____

_____

_____

_____

Notes

Entertainment

Band or DJ

Which One Is for You, a Band or DJ?

When making the decision whether to hire a band or DJ, keep several factors in mind. With a band, you are hiring professional musicians whose livelihood depends upon their music. This usually means they are responsible adults who will return phone calls and definitely show up for your affair! Bands, however, will generally cost you more than most DJs. Of course, the price varies depending on the number of musicians, reputation, and current popularity. Do keep in mind, though, that their rendition of your favorite songs may or may not sound similar to the originals you've been listening to on the radio. If you want original renditions, you should consider a DJ.

If you decide to use a DJ, there are large differences not only in price, but in professionalism. Sometimes the DJ may be just a young man spinning records to make some extra money on weekends. He will definitely charge you less, but he may not be as conscientious about returning phone calls or showing up the day of the affair! There are, though, some DJs who are extremely professional. It's their full-time job and they'll charge you accordingly. They can cost as much as, or more than, a band, depending on their use of light and sound effects, reputation, popularity, and cost of handouts. (I know one who gives out tickets to Mets games.)

Selecting the Band or DJ

Your selection of the band or DJ is one of the most important, and most difficult, decisions you'll need to make. It's difficult for two reasons. First, many bands will not allow you to listen to them play at someone else's affair. Second, you won't start going to many Bar and Bat Mitzvah celebrations (unless this is your second or third child) and develop a real sense of comparison until the year of your own child's Bar/Bat Mitzvah. By this time, it may be too late. Bands or DJs that are really good are often booked one to two years in advance.

When you do go to Bar and Bat Mitzvah celebrations each year, if you are like most of us, you probably don't pay that much attention to the music. You may remember if you liked it, but that's all. What you don't notice, but the host and hostess do, is how well the bandleader reads the crowd. In other words, when the children are eating, is the band playing "oldies" for the adults? Or, when the adults are eating, is the band playing games with the children? Does the band keep the children entertained the entire evening and the adults happy too? Does the soft dinner music start before all guests are served and last too long? All bands usually say they will play four hours of continuous music, but this may not mean what you have in mind. They'll have some dance music, then they'll take a break and leave one musician playing some music. This music, you may or may not like. How long are their breaks? Who is entertaining you during them? How can you avoid these pitfalls and not be disappointed?

To develop a sense of comparison you must closely observe the band at each affair you attend now. It is never too early to start looking and listening. Then, when you select a band, make sure that when you sign your contract and get references, you are getting the exact band you listened to and liked. Many people are shocked when the band that appears at their affair is not the exact same one they thought they'd hired! Some bands are notorious for having several bands under the same name. Check carefully that yours is not one of them. For example, hiring the Marty Nadler Band may not mean you are getting the Marty Nadler Band you observed. There may be numerous Marty Nadler Bands, each with a different leader and reputation.

Instructions to the Band

First, give them a timetable—a schedule of everything you're planning on the day of your affair. For example, you may want the challah blessing to be followed by the traditional hora at the beginning and the candle lighting near the end. Or perhaps you want all these events at the beginning because you know some people have to leave early. What music do you want during the candle-lighting ceremony? Do you want soft music or no music when your child speaks? Your bandleader needs to know these as well as your other preferences. Do you hate loud music or love it? Do you want the music to cater to the adults, the children, or both? Do you mind the children dancing to loud music while the adults are eating their dinner? Perhaps that is when you want the bandleader to be playing games with the children. Find out what games he has planned. You may also want him to plan the band's breaks according to the different courses being served. You should know how many breaks the band will take, how long these breaks will last, and what music to expect during them.

Don't knock yourself out making a list of the music you want to hear unless it's in your contract that they'll play it. I know many hosts and hostesses, myself included, who were made promises and spent lots of time making up lists of their favorite songs, only to be disappointed. Make sure the bandleader knows the proper pronunciation of everyone's name for the challah blessing and candle-lighting ceremony and whether or not you want music accompaniment. Also, find out if the band expects to be served dinner. They really needn't be if your affair is in the evening and starts at 8:00 p.m. Check with your caterer; some will charge you a minimum amount to serve your band, photographer, and videographer.

If you are having a female singer, you may want to inquire about her attire. More than one band has raised an eyebrow or two when the female singer comes inappropriately dressed for a Bar or Bat Mitzvah!

40

Cocktail Hour

Since guests will be greeting each other, chatting, and probably not dancing during cocktail hour, most hosts usually choose soft music or no music during this time. Bands and DJs usually charge you one price for four hours of entertainment, so you are better off paying just one musician for the cocktail hour music (e.g., piano, violin, or harp). After cocktails, the band or DJ can then start their four hours of music entertainment.

Payment

Usually a deposit is required in advance and final payment is made the day of the affair. Some bands insist on a certified check before they begin to play. I guess they suspect that if you're not happy, you may not pay them! I would insist on paying after the affair. It only makes sense that if they have to wait until the end of the affair for payment, they will keep trying to please you. They can't ignore, "You're playing too loud while we are eating" or "Stop all those breaks and the mellow music, we want to dance." If they haven't been paid, it's the only bargaining tool you'll have.

If you want more than four hours, look at your contract closely; that extra hour will cost you dearly! Personally, if your guests want to stay longer, I feel you have no choice but to hire the band for that extra hour. Be wary of the band that picks up the pace of the music in the last half hour before their time to end draws near, tricky-tricky!!

Band/DJ Possibilities*

Name:_____

Address: _____

Telephone: _____

Time Available:_____

Manager: _____

Number of Musicians: _____

Male/Female Singer Attire: _____

Instruments: _____
_____

Type of Music: _____
_____

Number of Breaks:_____

Length of Breaks: _____

Music during Breaks: _____

Audition date: _____

Games for Children: _____
_____

Prizes or Handouts: _____
_____

Cost: _____

Deposit Due/Refundable: _____

Balance Due:_____

Overtime Costs: _____

References: _____
_____
_____

*For your convenience, duplicate forms are included for
each of your interviews with bands/DJs.

Band/DJ Possibilities

Name:_____

Address: _____

Telephone: _____

Time Available:_____

Manager: _____

Number of Musicians: _____

Male/Female Singer Attire: _____

Instruments: _____

_____

Type of Music: _____

_____

Number of Breaks:_____

Length of Breaks: _____

Music during Breaks: _____

Audition date: _____

Games for Children: _____

_____

Prizes or Handouts: _____

_____

Cost: _____

Deposit Due/Refundable: _____

Balance Due:_____

Overtime Costs: _____

References: _____

_____

_____

Band/DJ Possibilities

Name:_____

Address: _____

Telephone: _____

Time Available:_____

Manager: _____

Number of Musicians: _____

Male/Female Singer Attire: _____

Instruments: _____
_____

Type of Music: _____
_____

Number of Breaks:_____

Length of Breaks: _____

Music during Breaks: _____

Audition date:_____

Games for Children: _____
_____

Prizes or Handouts:_____
_____

Cost: _____

Deposit Due/Refundable: _____

Balance Due:_____

Overtime Costs: _____

References: _____
_____
_____

Band/DJ Possibilities

Name:_____

Address: _____

Telephone: _____

Time Available:_____

Manager: _____

Number of Musicians: _____

Male/Female Singer Attire: _____

Instruments: _____

_____

Type of Music: _____

_____

Number of Breaks:_____

Length of Breaks: _____

Music during Breaks: _____

Audition date:_____

Games for Children: _____

_____

Prizes or Handouts: _____

_____

Cost: _____

Deposit Due/Refundable: _____

Balance Due:_____

Overtime Costs: _____

References: _____

_____

_____

Band/DJ Possibilities

Name:_____

Address: _____

Telephone: _____

Time Available:_____

Manager: _____

Number of Musicians: _____

Male/Female Singer Attire: _____

Instruments: _____

_____

Type of Music: _____

_____

Number of Breaks:_____

Length of Breaks: _____

Music during Breaks: _____

Audition date: _____

Games for Children: _____

_____

Prizes or Handouts: _____

_____

Cost: _____

Deposit Due/Refundable: _____

Balance Due:_____

Overtime Costs: _____

References: _____

_____

_____

Band/DJ Possibilities

Name:_____

Address: _____

Telephone: _____

Time Available:_____

Manager: _____

Number of Musicians: _____

Male/Female Singer Attire: _____

Instruments: _____

_____

Type of Music: _____

_____

Number of Breaks:_____

Length of Breaks: _____

Music during Breaks: _____

Audition date:_____

Games for Children: _____

_____

Prizes or Handouts: _____

_____

Cost: _____

Deposit Due/Refundable: _____

Balance Due:_____

Overtime Costs: _____

References: _____

_____

_____

Entertainment

Try to get a list of games the band or DJ will be playing with the children. If this is the twentieth party the kids have attended, try to come up with something original. It's definitely a disadvantage having a son or daughter born later in the year and having lots of friends with Bar and Bat Mitzvahs before theirs. A game such as Coke and Pepsi is fun the fifth time, but not necessarily as entertaining the twentieth time! Also, ask the band or DJ whether they are handing out prizes to the winners of the games. If not, you may want to provide something yourself (e.g., records). Be suspicious when a band or DJ can't give you a list of games. It may mean that they are not used to entertaining lots of children and may not be the band or DJ for you. Playing for wedding guests is entirely different from playing for Bar or Bat Mitzvah guests.

If you are having many children, you may want to consider some form of entertainment besides the band. The band can put you in touch with a company that books various entertainment acts. Don't be too shocked at the expense! This is just one of many items that can raise the cost of your party. You may, however, decide that it's worth the price, especially if you think the children won't be dancing, your band doesn't play games with them, or the band will be catering mostly to the adults. Also, you may be concerned that if the children aren't kept busy, they may get into mischief. This can and does happen.

There are some ways to cut down on entertainment costs. If you don't use one of the entertainment booking agencies, you can save a lot. Keep in mind that local college talent often goes untapped. Go to a local art store. Generally, the salespeople are art students themselves or know an art student who is good at caricatures. Then, get this caricaturist to do the children's faces on T-shirts or paper and use this as their favor. Also, consider getting an enthusiastic graduate student majoring in music to play the piano for your cocktail hour. An extra hour of playing can be very costly; a band hires only union members. They can't complain, though, if it's a friend or your cousin Mark!

Remember that when you book certain entertainers, they will be periodically removing guests from the party. For example, a magician is fine during cocktail hour but a caricaturist can do only about ten portraits an hour. This means that during cocktail hour, only ten children will have their portraits done. It's fine if you need the kids to be entertained and the band is not sufficient. However, if you want everyone to be dancing and mingling the entire time, you may want to avoid this type of entertainment. Possible entertainment you may want to consider includes carnival games, computer portraits, face painters, impersonators, mentalists, mini-music studio, pose with the stars, psychics, fortune tellers, robots, stilt walkers, and video games.

48

Favors

Put your walking shoes on and get going! It's really difficult to find a favor that you think both boys and girls will like, will keep, will use, and that won't be too childish. Most of all it needs to be something that your son or daughter will approve! Here are some examples of favors which my son received: T-shirts, boxer shorts, slippers, water spritzers, stuffed animals, banks, and calculators. Since you may be ordering a large number, you can save a lot by ordering early and directly from the manufacturer. Usually the manufacturer's name and address is somewhere on the product you are considering. Make sure you order way in advance; give them enough time in case they are late with delivery. The last thing you need is 40 of anything delivered after the party!

One way to kill two birds with one stone is by having the favor provided by some entertainer: for example, as mentioned before, the caricaturist who does caricatures of the children, the artist who does air-brush designs on T-shirts, the photographer who puts instant photos on buttons or the videographer who tapes the children lip-synching to their favorite song. These are just some of numerous possibilities.

Other items that you may consider having at your party include: glowing necklaces, bracelets, bow ties, earrings, goo-goo eyes, straw eyeglasses, or colorful glow wigs. These items can be handed out by a member of the band to your guests. If you want to order these types of party items in large quantities, you can. There are catalogue companies, like the Oriental Trading Company (800-327-9678) or Sherman Specialty Company (800-645-6513), who will happily sell to you directly. You can then avoid ordering from the decorator or band and paying premium prices! Your friends who are teachers or dentists may know of a catalogue company to suggest. They may get these catalogues from companies trying to sell small children's toys (the type a doctor might hand out to his young patients on their office visits). Then, you can just call to receive a copy of the catalogue. Start early to locate items at discount prices. A local gift shop may also be helpful.

Don't forget about wrapping the favors you are giving. Perhaps you want them in a colorful shopping bag or in colorful cellophane tied with ribbons. You can use the favors for seating assignments by placing them at each child's place setting. Paper goods, ribbons, balloons, etc., can also be found at discount (e.g., from Straus Company in Port Chester, New York).

Favors Checklist

Possibilities	Cost Per Item

Where to Shop	Done

Final Decision	Cost Per Item	Number to Order

Where Purchased	Date Delivered	Total Cost

Photography/Videography

Photographer/Videographer

Video or Photography, Which One Is for You?

Perhaps you should use both! If you can afford to, I would. This is not the place to cut corners because it's pictures that will recapture that special day for you years later. There are some ways to cut the corners a bit, though; read on.

Selecting the Photographer

Many photographers will insist that you buy a package consisting of an album of 24 or 36 8"x10"s with some additional photos included. This can turn out to be quite costly for a limited selection of pictures. While some photographers will not sell you the negatives, they may be willing to negotiate some package that includes the proofs, consisting of one shot of every picture taken. The best way to save money with a photographer is to find one who will sell you the proofs alone. Then you can make your own album. In addition, you can have a few pictures blown up for framing for yourself and relatives.

Take the time to check out several photographers. They can really vary in price and quality. Some are better at portraits but not very good at candid shots. Of course, you want one that takes sharp, clear pictures and is good at both. Examine their photographs of someone else's Bar or Bat Mitzvah before making your decision. Look to see that the photographer you planned on using doesn't take too many head-to-foot shots, takes enough close-ups, and includes plenty of candids.

Instructions to the Photographer

I prefer a photographer who is totally unobtrusive, someone who blends in with the guests as much as possible. If you agree, ask a reference about this. Tell the photographer exactly the photos you want taken. Are there special relatives or friends you want shots of together? Do you want many photographs of the children? I recommend individual table shots because they are your only complete record of your guests; not everyone is on the dance floor, where the photographer may be most of the time.

Suggestions

Get references on every photographer you're considering. The best references are those from friends who share your taste. Meet the photographer at an earlier date or time before the service to take all formal temple shots and portraits with your immediate family, grandparents, and rabbi. By taking these family pictures early, you will be able to spend more time with your guests both after the service and during the party. Remember, flashes are usually not allowed in temple during the service.

Payment

It is customary to give the photographer a deposit, often one-half the total, to reserve the date. The balance is then paid on delivery of your photographs.

Selection of Videographer

I think having someone take a video of both your service and reception is worth every penny. If you have experienced an obtrusive videographer, you will definitely disagree with me here. So just shop around until you find one that suits your individual taste. Believe me, you will be so happy years later when you can look back and see your friends, relatives, and your son's or daughter's friends at your affair. You'll have the opportunity to relive that joyous day over and over again.

There is a tremendous range in price for videographers. You can hire an amateur very inexpensively. Of course, it'll be an unedited version, quite lengthy, and something only your nearest and dearest will ever sit all the way through. But this may be all you'll need to relive that special day. Or, for a lot more money, you can have a polished, edited version with music and special effects. Prices and quality vary tremendously. Pick someone whose work you've seen and really like.

Instructions to Videographer

Your video company should be familiar with your temple. They probably will be if you hire a local company. If not, make sure they test for a clear audio (sound) from where they will be taking the pictures. Sometimes, they can attach a hidden microphone at the bimah, if your rabbi does not object. It would be a shame to discover after the service that while the pictures came out great, your son's or daughter's voice was too low to be picked up by a microphone in the rear of the temple. You will have to decide if you like the idea of on-camera interviews during the reception. Some people hate the idea of a cameraman giving their guests a microphone and asking them to speak. I was one of them. However, friends who have already had a video made may tell you otherwise; candid interviews can be the best part. A compromise may be your having just the children's comments (I did this!). Your son or daughter will love it five years from now.

Payment

Usually you give one-third of the payment to reserve the date, one-third the day of the affair, and one-third upon delivery. The price may include not just the edited version, but also an unedited version of the entire service and reception. Make sure you know exactly what you will be receiving for the amount charged and when it'll be delivered. Also, if you want copies (it's a pain to make your own since you need two VCRs to do it), you may want to have these included in the initial price or at least find out how much they'll be.

Photographer Possibilities*

Name of Studio: _____

Address: _____

_____

Telephone: _____

Name of Specific Photographer: _____

Name of Assistant for Lighting: _____

Time Available for Services: _____

Time Available for Reception: _____

Number of Proofs: _____

Cost of Proofs: _____

Proof Delivery Date: _____

Cost of Album: _____

Album Delivery Date: _____

Various Package Plans Available: _____

_____

_____

_____

Cost/Extra Photos/Sizes: _____

_____

_____

References: _____

_____

_____

*For your convenience, duplicate forms are included for
each of your interviews with photographers.

Photographer Possibilities

Name of Studio: _____

Address: _____

_____

Telephone: _____

Name of Specific Photographer: _____

Name of Assistant for Lighting: _____

Time Available for Services: _____

Time Available for Reception: _____

Number of Proofs: _____

Cost of Proofs: _____

Proof Delivery Date: _____

Cost of Album: _____

Album Delivery Date: _____

Various Package Plans Available: _____

_____

_____

_____

Cost/Extra Photos/Sizes: _____

_____

_____

References: _____

_____

_____

Photographer Possibilities

Name of Studio: _____

Address: _____

_____

Telephone: _____

Name of Specific Photographer: _____

Name of Assistant for Lighting: _____

Time Available for Services: _____

Time Available for Reception: _____

Number of Proofs: _____

Cost of Proofs: _____

Proof Delivery Date: _____

Cost of Album: _____

Album Delivery Date: _____

Various Package Plans Available: _____

_____

_____

_____

Cost/Extra Photos/Sizes: _____

_____

_____

References: _____

_____

_____

Photographer Possibilities

Name of Studio: _____

Address: _____

_____

Telephone: _____

Name of Specific Photographer: _____

Name of Assistant for Lighting: _____

Time Available for Services: _____

Time Available for Reception: _____

Number of Proofs: _____

Cost of Proofs: _____

Proof Delivery Date: _____

Cost of Album: _____

Album Delivery Date: _____

Various Package Plans Available: _____

_____

_____

_____

Cost/Extra Photos/Sizes: _____

_____

_____

References: _____

_____

_____

Photographer Possibilities

Name of Studio: _____

Address: _____

_____

Telephone: _____

Name of Specific Photographer: _____

Name of Assistant for Lighting: _____

Time Available for Services: _____

Time Available for Reception: _____

Number of Proofs: _____

Cost of Proofs: _____

Proof Delivery Date: _____

Cost of Album: _____

Album Delivery Date: _____

Various Package Plans Available: _____

_____

_____

_____

Cost/Extra Photos/Sizes: _____

_____

_____

References: _____

_____

_____

Videographer Possibilities*

Name of Studio: _____

Address: _____

Telephone: _____

Name of Specific Videographer: _____

Type of Camera (type of tape, wireless): _____

Name of Assistant for Lighting (unobtrusive): _____

Time Available for Services: _____

Time Available for Reception: _____

Length of Unedited Version: _____

Cost of Unedited Version: _____

Unedited Version Delivery Date: _____

Length of Edited Version: _____

Cost of Edited Version: _____

Edited Version Delivery Date: _____

Special Effects: _____

_____

_____

Music: _____

_____

_____

If Photos Used, Due Date: _____

Cost of Extra Copies: _____

References: _____

_____

_____

_____

*For your convenience, duplicate forms are included for
each of your interviews with videographers.

Videographer Possibilities

Name of Studio: _____

Address: _____

Telephone: _____

Name of Specific Videographer: _____

Type of Camera (type of tape, wireless): _____

Name of Assistant for Lighting (unobtrusive): _____

Time Available for Services: _____

Time Available for Reception: _____

Length of Unedited Version: _____

Cost of Unedited Version: _____

Unedited Version Delivery Date: _____

Length of Edited Version: _____

Cost of Edited Version: _____

Edited Version Delivery Date: _____

Special Effects: _____

_____

_____

Music: _____

_____

_____

If Photos Used, Due Date: _____

Cost of Extra Copies: _____

References: _____

_____

_____

_____

Videographer Possibilities

Name of Studio: _____

Address: _____

Telephone: _____

Name of Specific Videographer: _____

Type of Camera (type of tape, wireless): _____

Name of Assistant for Lighting (unobtrusive): _____

Time Available for Services: _____

Time Available for Reception: _____

Length of Unedited Version: _____

Cost of Unedited Version: _____

Unedited Version Delivery Date: _____

Length of Edited Version: _____

Cost of Edited Version: _____

Edited Version Delivery Date: _____

Special Effects: _____

_____

_____

Music: _____

_____

_____

If Photos Used, Due Date: _____

Cost of Extra Copies: _____

References: _____

_____

_____

_____

Videographer Possibilities

Name of Studio: _____

Address: _____

Telephone: _____

Name of Specific Videographer: _____

Type of Camera (type of tape, wireless): _____

Name of Assistant for Lighting (unobtrusive): _____

Time Available for Services: _____

Time Available for Reception: _____

Length of Unedited Version: _____

Cost of Unedited Version: _____

Unedited Version Delivery Date: _____

Length of Edited Version: _____

Cost of Edited Version: _____

Edited Version Delivery Date: _____

Special Effects: _____

_____

_____

Music: _____

_____

_____

If Photos Used, Due Date: _____

Cost of Extra Copies: _____

References: _____

_____

_____

_____

Photographer/Videographer Checklist*

Posed Portraits before Service   Wish List

Bar/Bat Mitzvah Alone/Tallis _____

Bar/Bat Mitzvah without Tallis _____

Bar/Bat Mitzvah with Parents _____

Bar/Bat Mitzvah with Mother _____

Bar/Bat Mitzvah with Father _____

Bar/Bat Mitzvah with Siblings _____

Bar/Bat Mitzvah with Grandparents _____

Bar/Bat Mitzvah with Grandmothers _____

Bar/Bat Mitzvah with Grandfathers _____

Bar/Bat Mitzvah with Parents/Siblings _____

Bar/Bat Mitzvah with All Close Relatives _____

Bar/Bat Mitzvah with Rabbi _____

Bar/Bat Mitzvah at Bimah _____

_____

_____

_____

_____

_____

_____

_____

_____

_____

_____

_____

***Check off the ones you want, add your own, and give a
copy of this page to photographer and videographer.
Copies are included here for your convenience.**

Photographer/Videographer Checklist*

Photographs to Take during Reception	**Wish List**
Bar/Bat Mitzvah Entering Reception	
Bar/Bat Mitzvah Blowing Out Candles on Cake	
Bar/Bat Mitzvah Cutting Challah	
Bar/Bat Mitzvah Dancing with Parent	
Bar/Bat Mitzvah Dancing with Friends	
Bar/Bat Mitzvah Dancing Hora	
Family Dancing Hora	
Parents Dancing	
Siblings Dancing	
Grandparents Dancing	
Bar/Bat Mitzvah Dancing with Grandparents	
Bar/Bat Mitzvah with All Girlfriends	
Bar/Bat Mitzvah with All Boyfriends	
Bar/Bat Mitzvah with All Friends	
Photos of Every Table	
Mother/Father with Old Friends	
Decorations/Centerpieces	
Bar/Bat Mitzvah at Conclusion of Affair	

_____

_____

_____

_____

_____

_____

_____

*Check off the ones you want, add your own, and give a
copy of this page to photographer and videographer.
Copies are included here for your convenience.

Photographer/Videographer Checklist

Posed Portraits before Service   **Wish List**

Bar/Bat Mitzvah Alone/Tallis _____

Bar/Bat Mitzvah without Tallis _____

Bar/Bat Mitzvah with Parents _____

Bar/Bat Mitzvah with Mother _____

Bar/Bat Mitzvah with Father _____

Bar/Bat Mitzvah with Siblings _____

Bar/Bat Mitzvah with Grandparents _____

Bar/Bat Mitzvah with Grandmothers _____

Bar/Bat Mitzvah with Grandfathers _____

Bar/Bat Mitzvah with Parents/Siblings _____

Bar/Bat Mitzvah with All Close Relatives _____

Bar/Bat Mitzvah with Rabbi _____

Bar/Bat Mitzvah at Bimah _____

_____

_____

_____

_____

_____

_____

_____

_____

_____

_____

Photographer/Videographer Checklist

Photographs to Take during Reception   Wish List

Bar/Bat Mitzvah Entering Reception _____

Bar/Bat Mitzvah Blowing Out Candles on Cake_____

Bar/Bat Mitzvah Cutting Challah _____

Bar/Bat Mitzvah Dancing with Parent_____

Bar/Bat Mitzvah Dancing with Friends_____

Bar/Bat Mitzvah Dancing Hora_____

Family Dancing Hora _____

Parents Dancing_____

Siblings Dancing _____

Grandparents Dancing_____

Bar/Bat Mitzvah Dancing with Grandparents _____

Bar/Bat Mitzvah with All Girlfriends _____

Bar/Bat Mitzvah with All Boyfriends _____

Bar/Bat Mitzvah with All Friends _____

Photos of Every Table _____

Mother/Father with Old Friends_____

Decorations/Centerpieces_____

Bar/Bat Mitzvah at Conclusion of Affair _____

_____

_____

_____

_____

_____

_____

_____

Photographer/Videographer Checklist

Posed Portraits before Service   Wish List

Bar/Bat Mitzvah Alone/Tallis _____

Bar/Bat Mitzvah without Tallis _____

Bar/Bat Mitzvah with Parents _____

Bar/Bat Mitzvah with Mother _____

Bar/Bat Mitzvah with Father _____

Bar/Bat Mitzvah with Siblings _____

Bar/Bat Mitzvah with Grandparents _____

Bar/Bat Mitzvah with Grandmothers _____

Bar/Bat Mitzvah with Grandfathers _____

Bar/Bat Mitzvah with Parents/Siblings _____

Bar/Bat Mitzvah with All Close Relatives _____

Bar/Bat Mitzvah with Rabbi _____

Bar/Bat Mitzvah at Bimah _____

_____

_____

_____

_____

_____

_____

_____

_____

_____

_____

Photographer/Videographer Checklist

Photographs to Take during Reception   Wish List

Bar/Bat Mitzvah Entering Reception _____

Bar/Bat Mitzvah Blowing Out Candles on Cake_____

Bar/Bat Mitzvah Cutting Challah _____

Bar/Bat Mitzvah Dancing with Parent_____

Bar/Bat Mitzvah Dancing with Friends _____

Bar/Bat Mitzvah Dancing Hora_____

Family Dancing Hora _____

Parents Dancing_____

Siblings Dancing _____

Grandparents Dancing_____

Bar/Bat Mitzvah Dancing with Grandparents _____

Bar/Bat Mitzvah with All Girlfriends _____

Bar/Bat Mitzvah with All Boyfriends _____

Bar/Bat Mitzvah with All Friends _____

Photos of Every Table _____

Mother/Father with Old Friends_____

Decorations/Centerpieces_____

Bar/Bat Mitzvah at Conclusion of Affair _____

_____

_____

_____

_____

_____

_____

_____

Decorations

Decorations

Selection of Flowers/Balloons

Flowers or balloons, which one is for you? See the decorator's work beforehand and get firm prices for what you want. This is one area where you can spend or save a lot of money because prices vary enormously. Don't think balloons will necessarily cost you less. They can be quite elaborate and cost you as much as flowers. The minimum decorations you'll probably need are centerpieces for each adult table and several for the children's table, depending on the size. As you add on decorations for the ceiling, more elaborate decorations for the children's table (e.g., balloon arches), and decorations for the cocktail area, prices start to climb! In addition to decorations at the reception, you will need to have one large floral arrangement for the temple (some people have two arrangements, but be sure you are not blocking anything or anyone). You may even want a small floral arrangement in the ladies' room.

Instructions to Florist/Party Planner

Be very clear as to what you want; more is not always better. You may want to consider having a theme based upon your child's favorite hobby (e.g., sport, musical instrument). Get involved in color selection. For example, the bimah in your temple may be a very dark wood, the color of the walls rose, the carpet blue. This should be considered when selecting your floral arrangement. Also, arrange for delivery of your flowers to your temple on Friday; so that they can be enjoyed by your congregation at the Friday evening service. Don't forget to ask a friend with a station wagon or van to bring this floral arrangement to your reception after the Bar/Bat Mitzvah service.

When making color selection of decorations at your reception, consider color of napkins, tablecloths, walls, carpeting, and chairs. If you are using balloons as centerpieces, make sure you know what they'll be attached to at the center of each table, how big each balloon will be (9" or 11"), and how many will be at each table. You will need to tell the decorator in advance the exact number of tables and the number of arrangements you want on the children's table.

Decide on the time that the decorator will be arriving and the time they'll complete their work. This must be coordinated with your caterer so that no one is in anyone else's way. Needless to say, you don't want your guests arriving while work is still being done!

Payment

It is customary to give a deposit to reserve your date. The balance is usually paid on the day of the affair.

Sign-In Board

This is an item that many children request, and something you should consider. Most of their friends sign it, making it a great memento that they can keep forever as a remembrance of their big day. There are lots of varieties. You can usually have one made through your decorator or do it yourself (e.g.,using a blow-up of a photo). There is also a wide variety in price, depending on how elaborate you want it to be.

Place the sign-in board in a prominent place where there will always be a lot of people. Some children seem to think it's funny to draw a mustache on an old baby photo of your child and really ruin what would otherwise be a great keepsake. To prevent this, tape a piece of cellophane over the face. Don't forget to get an easel (most restaurants, clubs, and hotels have one) and attach several markers to it with ribbons. Have someone check a couple of times during the reception to make sure the markers are still there, and replace them if necessary; you want to give all your guests an opportunity to sign.

Decorator/Florist Possibilities*

Name:_____

Address: _____

Telephone: _____

Person You're Working with: _____

Centerpiece Possibilities: _____

_____

Cost of Centerpiece Possibilities: _____
    (You won't know number you'll need until a later date)

_____

Dais Possibilities: _____
    (You'll decide on number you want at a later date)

_____

Cost of Dais Possibilities: _____

_____

Cocktail Area Possibilities: _____

_____

Cost of Cocktail Area Possibilities: _____

_____

Temple Arrangement Possibilities:_____

_____

Cost of Temple Arrangement Possibilities: _____

_____

Arrival Time/Set-Up for Temple Arrangement: _____

Arrival Time/Set-Up and Completion for Reception: _____

References: _____

_____

_____

_____

***For your convenience, duplicate forms are included for
each of your interviews with decorators/florists.**

Decorator/Florist Possibilities

Name:_____

Address: _____

Telephone: _____

Person You're Working with: _____

Centerpiece Possibilities: _____

_____

Cost of Centerpiece Possibilities: _____
    (You won't know number you'll need until a later date)

_____

Dais Possibilities: _____
    (You'll decide on number you want at a later date)

_____

Cost of Dais Possibilities: _____

_____

Cocktail Area Possibilities: _____

_____

Cost of Cocktail Area Possibilities: _____

_____

Temple Arrangement Possibilities:_____

_____

Cost of Temple Arrangement Possibilities: _____

_____

Arrival Time/Set-Up for Temple Arrangement: _____

Arrival Time/Set-Up and Completion for Reception: _____

References: _____

_____

_____

_____

Decorator/Florist Possibilities

Name:_____

Address: _____

Telephone: _____

Person You're Working with: _____

Centerpiece Possibilities: _____

_____

Cost of Centerpiece Possibilities: _____
    (You won't know number you'll need until a later date)

_____

Dais Possibilities: _____
    (You'll decide on number you want at a later date)

_____

Cost of Dais Possibilities: _____

_____

Cocktail Area Possibilities: _____

_____

Cost of Cocktail Area Possibilities: _____

_____

Temple Arrangement Possibilities:_____

_____

Cost of Temple Arrangement Possibilities: _____

_____

Arrival Time/Set-Up for Temple Arrangement: _____

Arrival Time/Set-Up and Completion for Reception: _____

References: _____

_____

_____

_____

Decorator/Florist Possibilities

Name: _____

Address: _____

Telephone: _____

Person You're Working with: _____

Centerpiece Possibilities: _____
_____

Cost of Centerpiece Possibilities: _____
   (You won't know number you'll need until a later date)
_____

Dais Possibilities: _____
   (You'll decide on number you want at a later date)
_____

Cost of Dais Possibilities: _____
_____

Cocktail Area Possibilities: _____
_____

Cost of Cocktail Area Possibilities: _____
_____

Temple Arrangement Possibilities: _____
_____

Cost of Temple Arrangement Possibilities: _____
_____

Arrival Time/Set-Up for Temple Arrangement: _____

Arrival Time/Set-Up and Completion for Reception: _____

References: _____
_____
_____
_____

Decorator/Florist Possibilities

Name:_____

Address: _____

Telephone: _____

Person You're Working with: _____

Centerpiece Possibilities: _____

_____

Cost of Centerpiece Possibilities: _____
    (You won't know number you'll need until a later date)

_____

Dais Possibilities:_____
    (You'll decide on number you want at a later date)

_____

Cost of Dais Possibilities: _____

_____

Cocktail Area Possibilities: _____

_____

Cost of Cocktail Area Possibilities: _____

_____

Temple Arrangement Possibilities:_____

_____

Cost of Temple Arrangement Possibilities: _____

_____

Arrival Time/Set-Up for Temple Arrangement: _____

Arrival Time/Set-Up and Completion for Reception: _____

References: _____

_____

_____

_____

Decorator/Florist Final Decision

Florist/Decorator: _____

Address: _____

_____

Telephone: _____

Manager: _____

Date and Time for Temple Arrangement Delivery: _____

Date and Time for Reception Decorations Completed: _____

Description of Temple Arrangement: _____

Cost of Temple Arrangement:_____

Colors Selected for Temple Arrangement:_____

    Keeping in mind colors of temple walls: _____

                      bimah: _____

                      carpet: _____

                      pews: _____

Description of Cocktail Area Decorations: _____

_____

Cost of Cocktail Area Decorations: _____

Description of Dais Decorations:_____

_____

Cost of Dais Decorations: _____

Description of Centerpieces: _____

_____

Cost of Centerpieces:_____

Colors Selected for Reception Decorations: _____

    Keeping in mind colors of reception location walls:_____

                      chairs:_____

                      carpet: _____

                      tablecloths: _____

                      napkins:_____

                      china: _____

Deposit: _____

Balance Due: _____

Invitations

The Invitation

The invitations must be ordered ahead of time. I can't emphasize enough how much aggravation and stress you can avoid if you take care of most things well in advance. Errors do occur, no matter how careful you may be, and although companies are willing to correct mistakes, they do need time!

There are several places from which you can order invitations: department stores, private stationery shops, decorators, and florists. Also, there is usually someone locally who may operate an invitation business out of his or her home. Dealing with someone nearby, who may be able to give you as much as a 20% discount, can be a true joy. They usually don't mind if you take home their books of invitations a half dozen times. You and your family can then study them and make a final decision. In addition, a local vendor can warn you if the invitation you've selected closely resembles a neighbor's.

What to Order

The invitation, the envelope, the response set (reply card and envelope), the reception card, a direction card (if you want it printed, as opposed to something you type up yourself and photocopy), thank-you notes, place cards, guest towels, cocktail napkins, matches, and yarmulkes are all items which can be ordered. It is up to you whether you feel it's necessary to have your son's or daughter's name on place cards, guest towels, cocktail napkins, and matches. These come in assorted colors and styles. The expense is minor here, but it all adds up. For example, blank place cards are available at most card shops and most restaurants. Hotels and clubs have their own cocktail napkins. As for the yarmulkes, if your temple is reform, some people may not wear them, so having them customized is an expense you may decide to avoid.

Decisions to Make

1. Number of Invitations—Remember, you needn't order the same number of invitations as there are guests. Those guests living under the same roof need to receive only one invitation. However, make sure you order a sufficient number, especially of envelopes, since whoever addresses them may make mistakes. You don't want to be forced to order more at the last minute if you can avoid it.

2. What You're Saying—There are various ways to phrase the invitation. Usually a certain number of lines are included in the price and extra lines cost a bit more. You can get lots of ideas from looking at invitation books.

3. The Reception Card—You can have a separate card or include "reception following services at ..." on the invitation.

4. Typeface—There are many styles in both script and print. Also, decide if you want your son's or daughter's name enlarged on the invitation.

5. Paper—What color do you want? Do you want layers or a single sheet? How thick will it be (weight)? You don't want it flimsy. See a sample.

6. Envelope—What color do you want? Do you want a lining? What color lining?

7. Ink Color—There are many colors to consider.

8. Response Set—Some people, even those not interested in saving money, decide not to include a response set because they prefer people's personal response on personal stationery. Most, however, do include a printed response set with a stamped envelope. Also, decide if you want the return address to say "Two" Price Lane or "2" Price Lane. There are also numerous possibilities as to what the card says. Look through invitation books to get ideas. You might want to number the response cards on the back in an inconspicuous place. This way, if someone just says, "We can come!" and doesn't sign their name, you won't go crazy trying to identify the anonymous acceptance.

9. Stamps—You'll need them for both the invitation itself and for the inside response envelopes. Make sure you weigh the invitation. Usually, additional postage will be necessary if you are enclosing several cards. Also, you may want to use a special stamp (e.g., baseball, love). You can order these from the post office in advance.

10. Addressing the Envelopes—This is certainly a place where you can easily save some money. Consider addressing the invitations yourself or having a loved one do this for you, especially if they have great handwriting, like my mom. Otherwise, you will have to hire a calligrapher. A friend may be able to recommend someone or a local art store can sometimes recommend a college art student who does calligraphy. Of course, check out some of their samples and get references. Computers with laser printers can also be used to address envelopes. Be sure to check all invitations yourself in case there are errors that need to be corrected. Pens that have an ink color that matches your invitation can be used for addressing the envelopes. Remember to write the address in the center, not to the right, because the return address is on the envelope flap and not in the front left corner. Even if you ordered your invitation late, you can usually obtain the envelopes ahead of time so that you can begin addressing them right away.

11. When to Send Them Out—You should send them out six to eight weeks before your affair, with an RSVP date of three weeks before the affair. This gives you a week after the RSVP date to call anyone who hasn't responded.

Printer Possibilities*

Name:_____

Address: _____

_____

Telephone: _____

Salesperson: _____

Estimated Cost

(If you haven't decided on the number of invitations you'll need, pick any number and stick to it as you visit all the printers. This way you'll be able to compare the prices you're given.)

Invitations:_____

Envelopes: _____

Reception Cards:_____

Response Sets:_____

Thank-You Notes:_____

Directions: _____

Book/Style Number

Invitations:_____

Envelopes: _____

Reception Cards:_____

Response Sets:_____

Thank-You Notes:_____

Directions: _____

Delivery Date:_____

References: _____

_____

_____

*For your convenience, duplicate forms are included
for each of your interviews with printers.

Printer Possibilities

Name:_____

Address: _____

_____

Telephone: _____

Salesperson: _____

Estimated Cost

(If you haven't decided on the number of invitations you'll need, pick any number and stick to it as you visit all the printers. This way you'll be able to compare the prices you're given.)

Invitations:_____

Envelopes: _____

Reception Cards:_____

Response Sets:_____

Thank-You Notes:_____

Directions: _____

Book/Style Number

Invitations:_____

Envelopes: _____

Reception Cards:_____

Response Sets:_____

Thank-You Notes:_____

Directions: _____

Delivery Date:_____

References: _____

_____

_____

_____

Printer Possibilities

Name:_____

Address: _____

_____

Telephone: _____

Salesperson: _____

Estimated Cost ·

(If you haven't decided on the number of invitations you'll need, pick any number and stick to it as you visit all the printers. This way you'll be able to compare the prices you're given.)

Invitations:_____

Envelopes: _____

Reception Cards:_____

Response Sets:_____

Thank-You Notes:_____

Directions: _____

Book/Style Number

Invitations:_____

Envelopes: _____

Reception Cards:_____

Response Sets:_____

Thank-You Notes:_____

Directions: _____

Delivery Date:_____

References: _____

_____

_____

_____

Printer Final Decision

Name:_____

Address: _____

_____

Telephone: _____

Salesperson: _____

	Invitations	Envelopes	Reception Cards
Cost			
Number Ordered			
Book/Style No.			
Typeface			
Ink Color			
Color/Layers			
Envelopes/Lining			
Date Ordered			
Delivery Date			

	Response Sets	Thank-you Notes	Directions
Cost			
Number Ordered			
Book/Style No.			
Typeface			
Ink Color			
Color/Layers			
Envelopes/Lining			
Date Ordered			
Delivery Date			

Wording for Printed Matter

Invitation

_____

_____

_____

_____

_____

_____

_____

_____

_____

_____

_____

_____

_____

_____

_____

_____

_____

_____

_____

_____

_____

_____

_____

Wording for Printed Matter

Envelopes (e.g., "14" or "Fourteen" Perdue Lane)

_____

_____

_____

_____

_____

_____

Reception Card

_____

_____

_____

_____

_____

_____

_____

Response Card

_____

_____

_____

_____

_____

_____

_____

Wording for Printed Matter

Directions or Map to Temple

_____

_____

_____

_____

_____

_____

_____

_____

_____

Wording for Printed Matter

Directions or Map to Reception

_____

_____

_____

_____

_____

_____

_____

_____

_____

_____

Invitation and Gift List*

Date Sent	Guest's Name Street Address City, State, Zip Code	Response			Gift Received	Thank You Note
		Yes	No	How Many?		

*You may want to write each name on a separate index card instead. This works well also, especially when you are giving your child thank-you notes to write each night.

Invitation and Gift List

Date Sent	Guest's Name Street Address City, State, Zip Code	Response			Gift Received	Thank You Note
		Yes	No	How Many?		

Invitation and Gift List

Date Sent	Guest's Name Street Address City, State, Zip Code	Response			Gift Received	Thank You Note
		Yes	No	How Many?		

Invitation and Gift List

Date Sent	Guest's Name Street Address City, State, Zip Code	Response			Gift Received	Thank You Note
		Yes	No	How Many?		

Invitation and Gift List

Date Sent	Guest's Name Street Address City, State, Zip Code	Response			Gift Received	Thank You Note
		Yes	No	How Many?		

Invitation and Gift List

Date Sent	Guest's Name Street Address City, State, Zip Code	Response			Gift Received	Thank You Note
		Yes	No	How Many?		

Invitation and Gift List

Date Sent	Guest's Name Street Address City, State, Zip Code	Response			Gift Received	Thank You Note
		Yes	No	How Many?		

Invitation and Gift List

Date Sent	Guest's Name Street Address City, State, Zip Code	Response			Gift Received	Thank You Note
		Yes	No	How Many?		

Invitation and Gift List

Date Sent	Guest's Name Street Address City, State, Zip Code	Response			Gift Received	Thank You Note
		Yes	No	How Many?		

Invitation and Gift List

Date Sent	Guest's Name Street Address City, State, Zip Code	Response			Gift Received	Thank You Note
		Yes	No	How Many?		

Invitation and Gift List

Date Sent	Guest's Name Street Address City, State, Zip Code	Response			Gift Received	Thank You Note
		Yes	No	How Many?		

Invitation and Gift List

Date Sent	Guest's Name Street Address City, State, Zip Code	Response			Gift Received	Thank You Note
		Yes	No	How Many?		

Invitation and Gift List

Date Sent	Guest's Name Street Address City, State, Zip Code	Response			Gift Received	Thank You Note
		Yes	No	How Many?		

Invitation and Gift List

Date Sent	Guest's Name Street Address City, State, Zip Code	Response			Gift Received	Thank You Note
		Yes	No	How Many?		

Invitation and Gift List

Date Sent	Guest's Name Street Address City, State, Zip Code	Response			Gift Received	Thank You Note
		Yes	No	How Many?		

Invitation and Gift List

Date Sent	Guest's Name Street Address City, State, Zip Code	Response			Gift Received	Thank You Note
		Yes	No	How Many?		

Invitation and Gift List

Date Sent	Guest's Name Street Address City, State, Zip Code	Response			Gift Received	Thank You Note
		Yes	No	How Many?		

Invitation and Gift List

Date Sent	Guest's Name Street Address City, State, Zip Code	Response			Gift Received	Thank You Note
		Yes	No	How Many?		

Invitation and Gift List

Date Sent	Guest's Name Street Address City, State, Zip Code	Response			Gift Received	Thank You Note
		Yes	No	How Many?		

Invitation and Gift List

Date Sent	Guest's Name Street Address City, State, Zip Code	Response			Gift Received	Thank You Note
		Yes	No	How Many?		

Hotel Arrangements for Out-of-Town Guests*

Hotel: _____

Address: _____

_____

Telephone: _____

Manager: _____

Total Number of Rooms: _____

Cost per Room per Night:_____

Date Reservation Made	Guest's Name	Number of Rooms	Dates

*Guests usually pay the cost of accommodations.
You can often obtain a group rate if many guests
stay at the same hotel.

Hotel Arrangements for Out-of-Town Guests

Hotel: _____

Address: _____

_____

Telephone: _____

Manager: _____

Total Number of Rooms: _____

Cost per Room per Night: _____

Date Reservation Made	Guest's Name	Number of Rooms	Dates

Hotel Arrangements for Out-of-Town Guests

Hotel: _____

Address: _____

_____

Telephone: _____

Manager: _____

Total Number of Rooms: _____

Cost per Room per Night: _____

Date Reservation Made	Guest's Name	Number of Rooms	Dates

Hotel Arrangements for Out-of-Town Guests

Hotel: _____

Address: _____

_____

Telephone: _____

Manager: _____

Total Number of Rooms: _____

Cost per Room per Night: _____

Date Reservation Made	Guest's Name	Number of Rooms	Dates

Transportation Arrangements for Guests*

Company: _____

Address: _____

_____

Telephone: _____

Manager: _____

Total No. of Guests Needing Transportation: _____

Cost: _____

Guest's Name	Transportation Provided By	Telephone Number

*Transportation to the temple and reception may have to be provided for some out-of-town guests. Children attending without parents will also need transportation between the temple and reception location. You can make arrangements with other guests to help, or hire a private company to provide transportation via van, limo, or bus.

Transportation Arrangements for Guests

Company: _____

Address: _____

_____

Telephone: _____

Manager: _____

Total No. of Guests Needing Transportation: _____

Cost: _____

Guest's Name	Transportation Provided By	Telephone Number

Transportation Arrangements for Guests

Company: _____

Address: _____

_____

Telephone: _____

Manager: _____

Total No. of Guests Needing Transportation: _____

Cost: _____

Guest's Name	Transportation Provided By	Telephone Number

Transportation Arrangements for Guests

Company: _____

Address: _____

_____

Telephone: _____

Manager: _____

Total No. of Guests Needing Transportation: _____

Cost: _____

Guest's Name	Transportation Provided By	Telephone Number

Transportation Arrangements for Guests

Company: _____

Address: _____

_____

Telephone: _____

Manager: _____

Total No. of Guests Needing Transportation: _____

Cost: _____

Guest's Name	Transportation Provided By	Telephone Number

Transportation Arrangements for Guests

Company: _____

Address: _____

_____

Telephone: _____

Manager: _____

Total No. of Guests Needing Transportation: _____

Cost: _____

Guest's Name	Transportation Provided By	Telephone Number

Clothing

Clothing

Since this is a special day for your entire family, you'll all want something special to wear. Mothers should begin looking for their dress immediately. If the affair is not formal, the father may want to select a new suit or new tie too. Unless you both expect drastic weight changes, there is no excuse not to get going. Remember, it's never too early to begin the march to the stores! It's a lot more enjoyable if you are not at the panicky, "I've got three weeks to get my dress " stage. Of course, you may have to wait a bit since stores sometimes don't stock their complete line of spring merchandise until late winter, or their fall merchandise until late summer. Since children are continually growing, I would suggest not buying their clothing too early. My son grew 3½ inches the summer before his Bar Mitzvah in October. Our pediatrician says that this is not unusual.

Don't forget that your child will need a tallis and yarmulke. If your temple doesn't have a gift shop or can't order these items for you, you can usually find them at another temple in your area. There is quite a variety so try to have your child with you when you make a selection.

For the Women

Department stores are a good place to begin. Even if you're not successful here, you'll get a good idea of the prices and styles available. You'll also become aware of which dresses are common. This is an important consideration because you definitely don't want to see your dress or your daughter's dress being worn by someone else at your affair. Next, by asking relatives and friends, make a list of all other stores to try. Needless to say, it's a real plus if you find a dress in a local store. It's a lot easier going back to a local store for fittings or to correct a problem than to a store an hour or more away. If you are unlucky in finding a local store, you will have to expand your search further. Again, use friends and relatives for tips on where to shop in their area. They'll know where you can get the best buy, where the prices are outrageous, and where they've been successful on previous shopping trips. Be sure to consider bridal shops. Usually, prices are a lot more reasonable there than at most small stores specializing in formal wear. A "Mother of the Bride" or even a sophisticated bridesmaid dress may be a possibility for a mother of the Bar Mitzvah boy or Bat Mitzvah girl.

When deciding what to wear, keep in mind whether your affair is in the evening or afternoon. Will you have time to change clothes between the service and the reception? A black strapless gown would no doubt be inappropriate if you'll be going up to the Bimah, unless you have some type of jacket or shawl to cover your shoulders.

It's a nice idea to touch base with grandmothers and aunts who will be in family pictures. You can't specify what color dresses they should wear, but if they are selecting something new or are considering several, you could diplomatically make suggestions. Pictures in which the women are wearing different colored dresses or prints simply don't look as good as those in which there is some color coordination. (This is probably how bridal party color schemes originated.) So if an aunt asks your advice in deciding between two dresses, it's not a bad idea if the color of her dress blends well with yours.

For the Men

It isn't necessary for everyone to purchase new clothing, but the Bar Mitzvah boy should have a suit that fits just right. Very often sports jackets and suits are worn so seldom by young men that we often borrow them or get a hand-me-down. They may not fit perfectly, but since they are worn just a couple of times, we usually don't care. On this special day, however, a new suit may certainly be in order. Make sure that any suit you purchase is tailored perfectly. Small shops usually do this at no charge, but you'll pay top dollar for the suit. You may swallow hard when you see the prices (a father's suit may cost less than a boy's suit), and don't expect discounts. Definitely consider department stores for large selections and possible sales. Also, the men's department will often tailor the suit if you've purchased it from the store's boys' department. You do have to ask for this service, which, although free, is not common knowledge!

Other men in the family may want to consider at least new ties for this special occasion. Don't forget to make sure that brothers' suits, sports jackets, and slacks fit also, since these are not the types of clothes boys wear every day, and they too are in those growing years. With all the other plans and arrangements it's easy to forget that brother Scott has also grown two inches this year. You don't want to become aware of little brother's extraordinary growth the night before your affair!

Shops to Visit

Women's	Done

Women's	Done

Men's	Done

Men's	Done

Shops to Visit

Girl's	Done

Girl's	Done

Boy's	Done

Boy's	Done

Mother's Attire Possibilities

Name of Store: _____

Address: _____

Telephone: _____

Salesperson: _____

Style Number: _____

Color: _____

Cost: _____

Alterations: _____

Date Ready: _____

Name of Store: _____

Address: _____

Telephone: _____

Salesperson: _____

Style Number: _____

Color: _____

Cost: _____

Alterations: _____

Date Ready: _____

Name of Store: _____

Address: _____

Telephone: _____

Salesperson: _____

Style Number: _____

Color: _____

Cost: _____

Alterations: _____

Date Ready: _____

Father's Attire Possibilities

Name of Store: _____

Address: _____

Telephone: _____

Salesperson: _____

Style Number: _____

Color: _____

Cost: _____

Alterations: _____

Date Ready: _____

_____

Name of Store: _____

Address: _____

Telephone: _____

Salesperson: _____

Style Number: _____

Color: _____

Cost: _____

Alterations: _____

Date Ready: _____

_____

Name of Store: _____

Address: _____

Telephone: _____

Salesperson: _____

Style Number: _____

Color: _____

Cost: _____

Alterations: _____

Date Ready: _____

Daughter's Attire Possibilities

Name of Store: _____

Address: _____

Telephone: _____

Salesperson: _____

Style Number: _____

Color: _____

Cost: _____

Alterations: _____

Date Ready: _____

_____

Name of Store: _____

Address: _____

Telephone: _____

Salesperson: _____

Style Number: _____

Color: _____

Cost: _____

Alterations: _____

Date Ready: _____

_____

Name of Store: _____

Address: _____

Telephone: _____

Salesperson: _____

Style Number: _____

Color: _____

Cost: _____

Alterations: _____

Date Ready: _____

Son's Attire Possibilities

Name of Store: _____

Address: _____

Telephone: _____

Salesperson: _____

Style Number:_____

Color: _____

Cost: _____

Alterations: _____

Date Ready:_____

_____

Name of Store: _____

Address: _____

Telephone: _____

Salesperson: _____

Style Number:_____

Color: _____

Cost: _____

Alterations: _____

Date Ready:_____

_____

Name of Store: _____

Address: _____

Telephone: _____

Salesperson: _____

Style Number:_____

Color: _____

Cost: _____

Alterations: _____

Date Ready:_____

Clothing Final Decisions

Mother's

Name of Store: _____

Address: _____

_____

Telephone: _____

Salesperson: _____

Style Number: _____

Color: _____

Cost: _____

Alterations: _____

Date Ready: _____

Father's

Name of Store: _____

Address: _____

_____

Telephone: _____

Salesperson: _____

Style Number: _____

Color: _____

Cost: _____

Alterations: _____

Date Ready: _____

Clothing Final Decisions

Daughter's

Name of Store: _____

Address: _____

_____

Telephone: _____

Salesperson: _____

Style Number: _____

Color: _____

Cost: _____

Alterations: _____

Date Ready: _____

Son's

Name of Store: _____

Address: _____

_____

Telephone: _____

Salesperson: _____

Style Number: _____

Color: _____

Cost: _____

Alterations: _____

Date Ready: _____

Family's Clothing and Accessory Checklist

	MOTHER	FATHER	DAUGHTER	DAUGHTER	DAUGHTER	SON	SON	SON
Dress								
Suit								
Sports Jacket								
Slacks								
Shirt								
Shoes								
Socks								
Stockings								
Tie/Bow Tie								
Pocketbook								
Coat								
Belt								
Suspenders								
Jewelry								
Cuff Links/Studs								
Hair Accessories								
Undergarments (e.g., strapless bra, slip)								

Temple Arrangements

Temple Services

Family's obligations vary according to each congregation. However, there are always certain duties you will be expected to do at the Bar/Bat Mitzvah service. The temple and rabbi will inform you of these in advance. Of course, if they haven't called you about one month before your date, call them.

Booklet

A personalized booklet is often handed out to your guests at the Bar/Bat Mitzvah service. This can be a small booklet and involve very little effort on your part or it can be much more elaborate and necessitate a real commitment from you. The best advice I can offer you here is to ask to see some of the booklets that have been used in your own temple and get a head start on whatever is expected of you.

Participation

The rabbi will ask you to give him the names of members of your family (usually the Hebrew names also) who will be participating in the Bar/Bat Mitzvah service. This usually involves some phone calls and some family discussion as to who is doing what. For example, for my son Dan's Bar Mitzvah, I needed to get: (1) someone to open the Ark; (2) two people to chant aliyot (a third is said by a parent and a fourth by the Bar/Bat Mitzvah child; you can have many more aliyot if you want); (3) someone to hold the Torah and someone to dress the Torah (These two people will be seated at the Bimah during your child's chanting of the Haftorah. They'll be seeing your child from the back, not the front. Thus, grandma might not like this role!). That's a total of five people that we needed to assist us during the service.

It's nice to have your immediate family participate. Grandmothers, grandfathers, uncles, aunts, and cousins are also very often asked. Sometimes, if you have a very small family, you might consider asking an old friend of the family or one of your child's close friends. Give a copy of the aliyah to all who will be chanting it. It makes everyone a lot less nervous if they know exactly what is expected of them.

The Bar/Bat Mitzvah Child

The rabbi will do everything possible to properly prepare the children for this special day. The more prepared they are, the less nervous they will be. The rabbi will probably also give them the opportunity to rehearse at the Bimah in the temple. This should help with any anxiety they may have. You can also have them practice in front of you or other members of the family. Have them rehearse reading the English portions also, reading clearly and slowly. We all tend to talk too rapidly when we are nervous. All this can help make them more comfortable when their big day arrives.

Since you will be busy making arrangements for the party, you may find yourself a bit anxious. Try not to pass this on to your child. Just remember who is coming to this celebration. It's your nearest and dearest. They'll love you even if the roast beef is cold or your child forgets a line. Relax and pass this advice on to your child.

The Parents

During the Bar/Bat Mitzvah service, you and your spouse will be asked to participate. You can divide your duties any way that you want. One can do the aliyah and the other the parents' prayer, or you can each do half of both. You may also be asked to take part in the Friday evening service if your child's Bar/Bat Mitzvah is on Saturday. The mother of the Bar/Bat Mitzvah child usually lights the candles and says the blessing. Temples vary tremendously as to how little or how much the parents take part in the service. Check to see what is customary at your temple.

Service Arrangements

Date: _____

Temple: _____

Address: _____

Telephone: _____

Manager: _____

Maximum Seating: _____

Starting Time: _____

Ending Time: _____

Colors of Temple Walls/Bimah/Carpet: _____

Type of Ceremony (A.M. or Havdalah): _____

Rabbi Meeting Date: _____

Person Opening Ark/Hebrew Name: _____

Person Holding Torah/Hebrew Name: _____

Person to Dress Torah/Hebrew Name: _____

People Chanting Aliyot/Hebrew Names: _____

_____

_____

_____

Choir/Cantor: _____

Person to Move Flowers to Reception:_____

Video Rules (e.g., not obvious, microphone hidden): _____

_____

Photographer Rules (e.g., not during service, no flash): _____

_____

Other: _____

_____

_____

_____

Family's Service Responsibilities

Bar/Bat Mitzvah Child's Responsibilities   **Done**

Practice Hebrew Readings: _____

Practice English Readings: _____

Write and Practice Speech: _____

Other: _____

Parents' Responsibilities   **Done**

Parents' Aliyah:_____

Parents' Prayer: _____

Individualize Booklet: _____

Ask Relative or Friend to Open Ark:_____

                                         Hold Torah: _____

                                         Dress Torah: _____

                                         Say Aliyah: _____

                                         Say Aliyah: _____

                                         Other (e.g., More Aliyot):_____

                                         _____

                                         _____

                                         _____

                                         _____

                                         _____

Get Hebrew Names of Those Participating: _____

Kiddush for All Those Attending Services:_____

Mother Lighting Candles at Friday Night Service: _____

Seating

Seating Plan

The first step in developing a seating plan is to decide on the size, shape, and arrangement of the tables. This will require some thinking! Where do you want the dais table (some prefer keeping children close to the band)? In what shape do you want the children's tables to be arranged (like an E, H, I, straight, or are you using round tables for the children too)? What sizes and number of tables do you need (e.g., six of the 60", three of the 72")? Usually the 60" tables seat eight to ten people and the 72" tables seat ten to twelve people. You usually won't have to tell the reception hall these specifics until a week before the affair, but if you need many large tables, some places will have to rent them.

The second step is to diagram the seating arrangement of your guests. For the children's seating arrangement, let your child do this, since he knows who is friendly with whom. One suggestion here is to seat children who know no one together. There is a better chance that they'll start a conversation with someone who also knows no one than if you sit them with children who all know each other very well. You don't need to give specific seat assignments to the adults; just a table number will do.

Finally, alphabetize your place cards and give them to the reception hall. Discuss where you want the place card table and how it should be decorated.

Seating Chart

Table 1	Table 2	Table 3	Table 4	Table 5

Table 6	Table 7	Table 8	Table 9	Table 10

Seating Chart

Table 11	Table 12	Table 13	Table 14	Table 15

Table 16	Table 17	Table 18	Table 19	Table 20

Seating Chart

Table 21	Table 22	Table 23	Table 24	Table 25

Table 26	Table 27	Table 28	Table 29	Table 30

Layout of Tables at Reception*

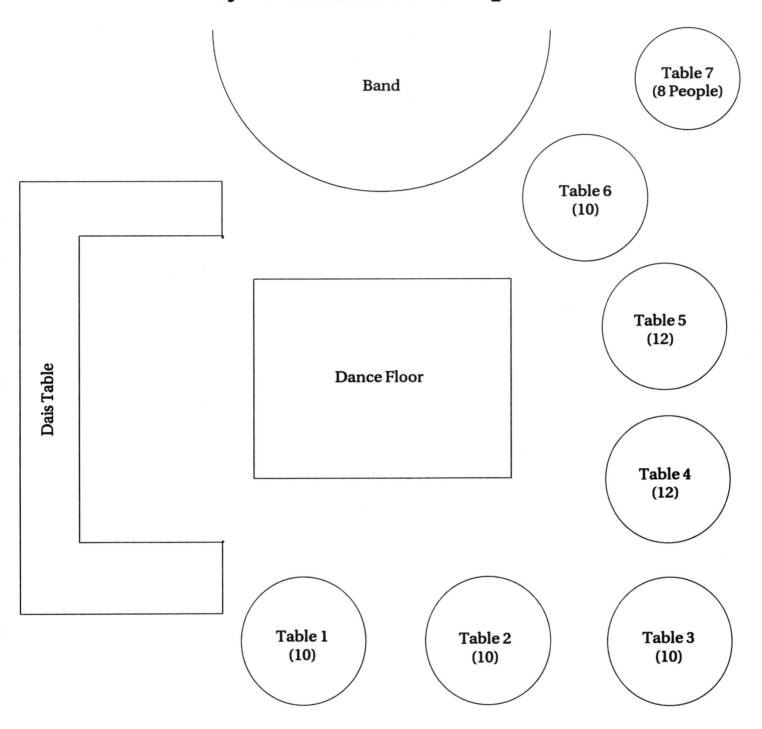

*This is just an example of what you need to do. Use the next page for your layout.

Layout of Tables at Reception

Possible Dais Arrangements

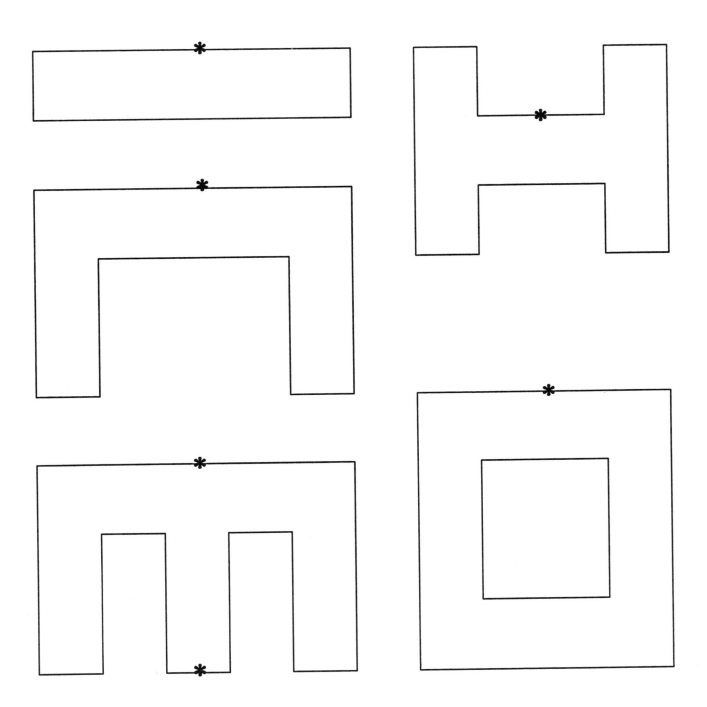

*Indicates where your child might be seated, so he or she
will be surrounded by the most friends.

Seating Assignments at Children's Dais Table*

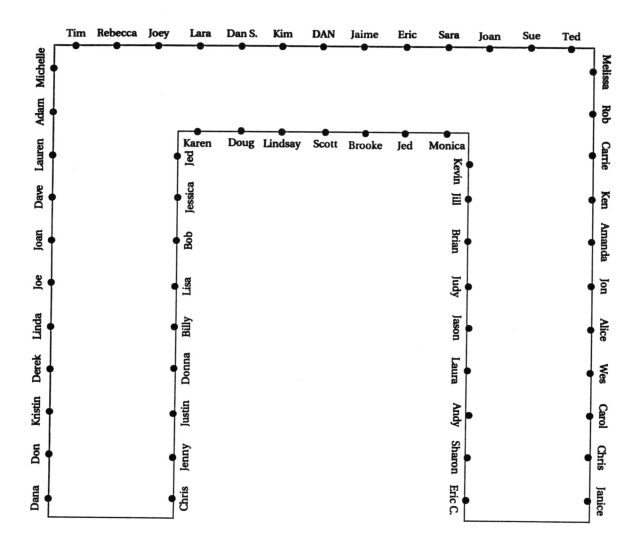

*This is just an example of what you need to do. Use the next page for your own dais seating assignments. Some people prefer to use round tables for the children also and give no specific seat assignment.

Seating Assignments at Children's Dais Table

Seating Assignments At Children's Dais Table

Budget

Budget and Gratuities

Budget

Description	Decision Made	Estimated Costs	Deposit Due	Balance Due
Reception Hall				
Caterer				
Music				
Entertainment				
Florist				
Party Planner				
Photographer				
Videographer				
Stationery				
Favors/Wrapping				
Cake				
Transportation				
Parking			—	—
Coat Room			—	—
Rentals				
Rabbi Gift			—	—
Choir Gifts			—	—
Family's Attire			—	—
Challah/Candles			—	—
Other Miscellaneous				
Gratuities	—		—	—
Tax	—		—	—
Total	—		—	—

Gratuities

Giving tips is not always optional as you might assume. Most caterers include a 15% to 20% gratuity in their per-person price for the meal, and this is something that you should inquire about at the start of your discussions. Some people have told me, however, that their caterer simply suggested a percentage, but this is more the exception than the rule.

There are times when tipping is optional. For example, many people tip the maître d' or catering manager, and the bartenders. The amount you decide to give is totally up to you and is not an amount based upon the cost of your entire affair. A tip is not usually expected by the band, DJ, videographer, photographer, printer, or decorator.

My final suggestion is that tipping be done at a time you feel would be most effective, thus assuring you the best possible service. This may mean tipping before your affair as opposed to after it. For example, saying to the bartender, as you hand him or her a tip, "please take good care of my guests," is very different from handing him or her a tip after the reception, which is more the customary sign of appreciation.